COURAGE
for the
Discouraged

five ways to overcome discouragement

GWEN ENGLAND

Foreword by Pastor Raymond England

Notes section provided
in the back of this book for your
convenience.
Trust me you'll want to take notes.
Jot down anything the Holy Spirit
whispers to you.
Grab a pen!

FOREWORD

I have been acquainted with the author since the day her mom and I brought her home from the hospital.
Gwen has always been full of life and abundant joy. But no one gets to go through this life without disappointments, and things that discourage us.

The only cure for discouragement is to be infused with new courage. Gwen has experienced first hand some of life's biggest disappointments but she has faced them with courage.

I am very proud of Gwen and her courage to keep going forward in spite of life's disappointments. I believe the principles she shares in this book will work for all of us.

Pastor Raymond England

Pastor Raymond England

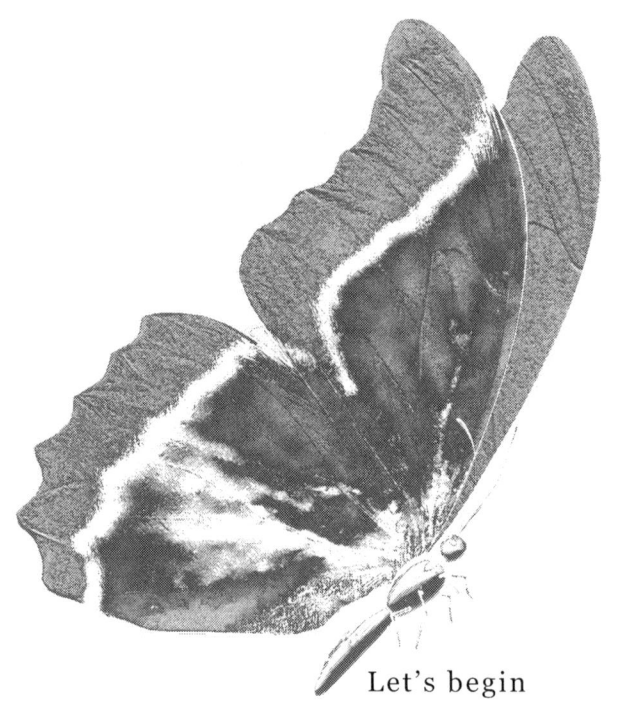

Let's begin

*This book is dedicated to my Heavenly Father.
I am so grateful to know Jesus.
He has made the difference in my life.*

*To my parents Raymond & Brenda England.
Thank you for everything you have done
to help me be where I am today. I love you.*

*To my best friend
Thank you for your gentle (and not so gentle) nudge
to write this book. Your faith and prayers propel me
forward as you continue to believe in me. I love you.*

*To the "Fabulous Four"
Thank you for your mentorship and friendship.
Your kindness refreshes my soul.*

*To Dr. Janet Faggart
Thank you for mentoring me and effortlessly exemplifying
how a godly woman thrives in ministry.*

Edited by Dr. Janet Faggart

Published By SW Publishing House

Why the butterfly? The butterfly holds special meaning for me as it was reminds me of my mother. But beyond that, the butterfly's fascinating life cycle perfectly captures the essence of this season. Emerging from a chrysalis, it undergoes a remarkable transformation, growing delicate wings. Any disruption to this process can have dire consequences, leading to injury, death, or a butterfly that is simply not as strong. For me the season of discouragement I endured has been an invitation from our Lord to help me become courages. Enjoy this book from yours truly, Courage for the Discouraged.

—Gwen

TABLE OF CONTENTS

Part 1 This Means War

Chapter 1 Satan's Weapon of Choice

Chapter 2 Wear Out The Saints

Chapter 3 Questioning God

Chapter 4 Side Effects of Discouragement

Part 2 Another Casualty of War

Chapter 5 Emotional Blowout

Chapter 6 Keep Hope Alive

Chapter 7 Discouragement's Hall of Fame

Chapter 8 Relationships: Who Said It's Not Personal?

Chapter 9 Circumstances Beyond Our Control

Part 3 Know Your Weapons

Chapter 10 Hope

Chapter 11 Prayer

Chapter 12 Praise

Chapter 13 Rest

Chapter 14 The Word of God

Part 4 God Ain't Finished

Chapter 15 Courage for the Discouraged

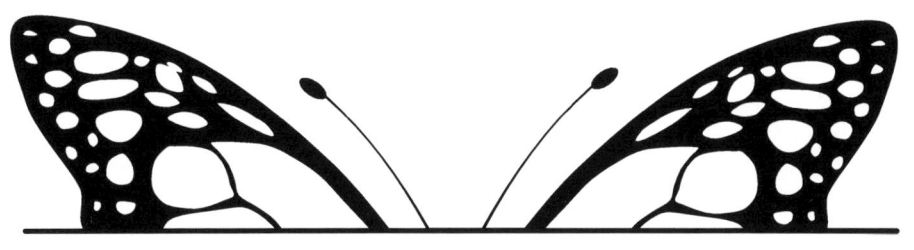

THIS MEANS WAR
PART ONE

Chapter 1
SATAN'S WEAPON OF CHOICE

"...and the soul of the people was much discouraged because of the way."
Numbers 21:4 KJV

Have you ever been disappointed with life? Have you ever questioned why things turned out the way they did? Have you ever had the courage to ask, "God, what are you doing? Why is this happening to me?"

If you are feeling overwhelmed, stressed out, anxious, and discouraged then this book is for you.

I never imagined myself as an author. It was a dear friend who encouraged me to write, suggesting it could be therapeutic for me. And honestly, it's my own disappointment with God that caused me to start writing this book. But it's His faithful love and overwhelming goodness that propelled me to finish it.

I hope that by the end of this book you are encouraged, equipped and more prepared to win the war against discouragement.

People have a tendency to underestimate the devastating effects of discouragement. We have minimized it and tried to brush it under the rug.

We often treat discouragement as though it's a small thing. We act like it's no big deal. But I have seen more people walk away from the Lord and walk away from church (not because of sin in their life) but because of discouragement. I have experienced firsthand the glaring devastation that discouragement leaves behind when it is not confronted properly.

I believe discouragement is the number one tool Satan uses to derail believers. Do you know at least one person who is not walking with the Lord today simply because they got discouraged?

There is an enemy waging war against our mental health. If we're going to win the war against discouragement, we better learn to use the weapons God has given us. Only God's strategy is effective when it comes to defeating the enemy's schemes.

It is my prayer that you will use this book to weaponize yourself and go into the battle better equipped so that you don't become discouragement's next casualty.
Armor up and grab your weapons, Here we go!

2 Corinthians 10:4 NIV
The weapons we fight with are not the weapons of the world. On the contrary, they have divine power to demolish strongholds.

Chapter 2
WEAR OUT THE SAINTS

"...And he (the enemy) will wear out the saints of the most High."
Daniel 7:25 ESV

As Christians, we have a tendency to hide behind comments like, "I'm doing good. Everything is good." But behind the 'good' facade our soul is discouraged.

There's a very revealing scripture in Numbers 21:4 KJV that says, "as they journeyed... the soul of the people was much discouraged because of the way."

Notice the last half of that verse, "and the soul of the people was much discouraged because of the way."

This verse is referring to the people of God (not the devil's crowd) that is discouraged.

Discouragement can be caused by a number of different things. (I will address a few of them later in this book.) But I want you to notice from this verse what caused their discouragement.

The Bible tells us they were discouraged "because of the way.'

I found that very interesting because God is the One leading the way. God is the One leading them by a cloud by day and a fire by night. Yet, they're discouraged because of the way.

Have you ever become discouraged in the ways of God?
Have you ever asked:
God, why are you leading me through this hot desert?
God, why is this journey taking so long?
God, is there not an easier, shorter way?

Scripture tells us that they became "much discouraged" because of the way God was leading them.

It is possible to be walking in the ways of God and still have to deal with discouragement.

No matter how long you've been saved, no matter how spiritually mature you are, we all go through seasons in our life where we become weary.

Daniel 7:25 ESV says, "...And he (the enemy) will wear out the saints of the most High."

Did you know you have an enemy? Scripture says he came to kill, steal and destroy (John 10:10 KJV). His ultimate goal is to destroy you. But if he can't take you out, then his next strategy is to wear you out.

Have you ever been worn out? Have you ever gotten so weary til your soul was tired? I'm not referring to the kind of tired where you can just take a nap and wake up feeling rested. I'm talking about has your soul ever felt weary and worn out? I found myself in this exact spot in the spring of 2024. I was so tired. In every aspect of my life I was exhausted. I was physically tired. I was emotionally tired. I was spiritually tired. I was worn out!

I was tired of doing the right thing.
I was tired of 'turning the other cheek'.
I was tired of honoring people who did not honor me back.
I was tired of giving more than I got.
I was tired of being overlooked.
And I was tired of pretending.

What are you tired of?

What has caused your soul to grow weary?

Are you tired of struggling with that addiction?

Are you tired of drowning in debt?

Are you tired of being stuck on a dead-end job?

Are you tired of being single? Tired of eating alone? Tired of sleeping alone?

Perhaps you're tired of being married.

Are you tired of picking up your husband's dirty socks and underwear off the floor?

Are you tired of your wife spending your money?

Are you tired of dealing with ungrateful and entitled kids?

Are you tired of your in-laws?

Are you tired of dealing with work issues that never get resolved?

The enemy's strategy is to wear out the saints. So, what has worn you out?

These little things accumulate over time until we find ourselves worn out. The pressures of life build up slowly and silently. Weariness and discouragement sneak in so subtly that we can reach a breaking point and not even know it until it's too late.

Since you're still reading this book, you may know exactly what I'm talking about.

You look good on the outside. You look like you're holding it all together. You're saying all the right things. And yet, the weariness of your soul and the pressure inside of you is so intense that the tip of your head is about to explode.

I've been there. Done that.

And that's exactly where the enemy wants you. His strategy is to wear out the saints.

Chapter 3
QUESTIONING GOD

"Are you the One? Are you the Messiah we've been expecting, or should we keep looking for someone else?"
Matthew 11:3 NLT

John the Baptist is a biblical example of a godly man who became discouraged. I want you to see how this story unfolds so you'll be aware of the enemy's strategy.

We jump into this story where John the Baptist has just baptized Jesus in the Jordan River.

John 1:32 NLT - Then John testified saying, "I saw the Holy Spirit descending like a dove from heaven and resting upon him." John 1:34 NLT - "I saw this happen to Jesus, so I testify that he is the Chosen One of God."

Then John boldly announces, "Behold, the Lamb of God, who takes away the sin of the world" John 1:29 KJV.

John had received a personal revelation and he knew beyond a doubt that Jesus was the Son of God. There was no question in his mind. He was confident that Jesus was the One true Messiah!

But John's confidence was short-lived.

Because a few chapters later we read that John is arrested, thrown in prison and placed on death row.

It's while John is wasting away in prison that he starts to lose his confidence. Discouragement sets in and he begins to doubt the very thing he used to be so sure of.

In Matthew 11:3 NLT, John sends a couple of messengers to ask Jesus, "Are you the One? Are you the Messiah we've been expecting, or should we keep looking for someone else?"

Notice in Matthew chapter 3 we see John confidently declaring, "Jesus is the Messiah". But eight chapters later John is not so sure anymore.

Do you see the danger of discouragement? It will cause you to question the very things that you previously affirmed about your faith in God.

John started second guessing himself. Did I really see the Holy Spirit descend on Jesus like a dove? Did I really hear a voice from heaven? Is Jesus really who he says he is?

It's easy to get discouraged and question your faith when you're being held captive in a prison.

You will encounter situations in your life that seem so unfair until you start to question your own faith. If Jesus is really who he says he is then why am I still stuck here in this prison cell? Why hasn't he rescued me?

In Matthew 11:11 NIV Jesus himself said, "Truly I tell you, among those born of women there has not risen anyone greater than John the Baptist."

And yet, this powerful prophet and anointed man of God is now doubting who Jesus is.

You will walk through seasons in your life where you don't see the Holy Spirit coming down from heaven like a dove anymore. All you see now is prison bars.

You'll go through seasons where you don't hear God's voice anymore. All you hear now is the sound of your rattling chains.

Unfair circumstances can cause such discouragement until you second guess who Jesus is.

Discouragement will also cause you to question the will of God and the love of God. If God loved me so much, why did he allow this to happen?

There are some things we will never have answers for. And when we dwell on those things and focus on those things we are creating an environment that is conducive for discouragement.

Chapter 4
SIDE EFFECTS OF DISCOURAGEMENT

Elijah went before the people and said, "How long will you waver between two opinions? If the LORD is God, follow him; but if Baal is God, follow him." But the people said nothing.
1 Kings 18:21 NIV

Throughout this book I want us to delve into different aspects of discouragement. I want us to look at the causes, the symptoms, the repercussions, and also how to fight against it.

Later on in the book, I'll also be sharing some of my own personal stories and experiences. But for now, let's look at five side effects of discouragement.

#1 Discouragement affects your vision.

Discouragement will make your spiritual vision blurry and unclear. Discouragement will try to convince you that you don't have a bright future. It wants you to believe that things will always appear to be dark and bleak and hopeless.

But I want to remind you of God's promise in Jeremiah 29:11 KJV, "God said, I know the plans I have for you. And they are plans to give you a hope and a future!"

#2 Discouragement will cause you to lose your passion, your excitement, and your enthusiasm for the presence of God.

Do you know people who used to be excited about being in the presence of God? They couldn't wait to get to church. They were the first ones there and the last ones to leave. But discouragement crept in… and now, they would just as soon stay in bed or go to the lake. Because discouragement caused them to lose their passion for the house of God.

David, the Psalmist said, "I was glad when they said unto me, let us go into the house of the Lord" (Psalm 122:1 KJV).

#3 Discouragement will cause you to isolate.

The devil wants to isolate you so he can devastate you. The enemy will do everything he can to pull you away from God's people. He'll try to isolate you from your family and friends. Don't fall prey to his tactics.

When you feel the least like going to church, that's a sign you need to be there the most.

When you feel the least like praising God,
that's when you need to praise Him the most.

Don't be ignorant of the enemy's strategy to isolate you. You are an easy target for the enemy when you isolate yourself. So, stay within the safety and covering of your Christian community.

#4 Discouragement Feeds Paralysis

Another sign of discouragement is paralysis. Satan uses discouragement to paralyze us so that we don't move forward.

When people are discouraged, they can't make clear decisive decisions. It's as though they're stuck. They're paralyzed. They can't seem to move forward.

1 Kings 18:21 KJV says, "Elijah approached all the people and said, 'How long will you halt between two opinions? If the Lord is God, follow Him; but if Baal, follow him.' But the people of Israel did not answer him so much as a word."

Discouragement will stop you from making choices that advance you and force you forward in life.
Discouragement will also silence you when you should be speaking up. Notice in the verse we just read that the people answered not a word.

Discouragement will try to stop you from moving forward and silence you from speaking up.

#5 Discouragement will affect your speech.

In the story I mentioned earlier in Numbers 21, the Israelites got discouraged and began to murmur and complain to Moses.

Discouragement will affect your speech. Your words become laced with sarcasm and negativity. You become judgmental and critical.

When the Israelites sent the twelve spies out to survey the Promised Land, ten of the spies returned with a negative report. Only two spies, out of ten, returned saying, "We can do this! Let's go in at once and conquer the city" (Numbers 13:30 KJV).

To my knowledge, that's the only time in the Bible where both groups were right.
The ten that said they couldn't, didn't.
The two that said they could, did.

Joshua and Caleb are the only two who had a good report and they're also the only two who received the Promise.

My point is this... the words that come out of your mouth determine what you can do and what you can't do.

And discouragement will always tell you that you can't do it. That's why the Bible says, let the weak SAY I am strong (Joel 3:10 KJV).

Discouragement is real! If you don't learn to fight it, it will overtake you.

If it can happen to John the Baptist, then it can happen to you and me.

That's why Isaiah 61:3 KJV says, we are to put on the garment of praise and take off the spirit of heaviness.

I love the Word of God. It paints a beautiful word picture that we have the option to choose which garment to wear. I pray you choose wisely to put on the garment of praise and take off the garment of heaviness.

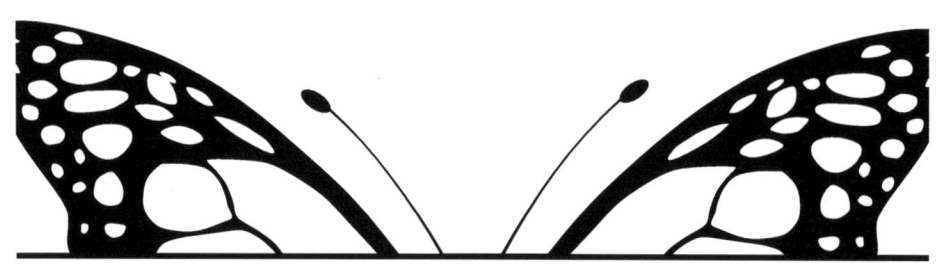
ANOTHER CASUALTY OF WAR
PART TWO
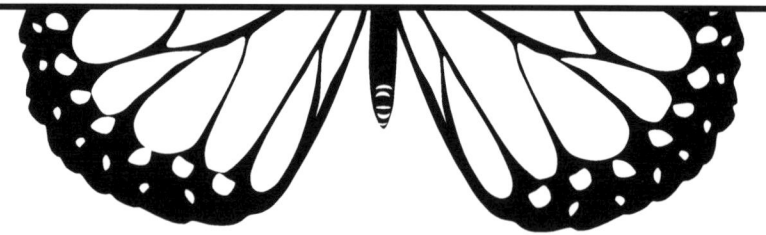

Chapter 5
EMOTIONAL BLOWOUT

*"When I am overwhelmed,
you alone know the way I should turn."
Psalm 142:3 NLT*

It was approximately 5:44 AM as I sat on the front porch drinking my coffee. It was still dark outside, but I knew within a few short moments the raging Texas sun would appear, and bring with it enough heat to literally suffocate me.

It was the 4th of July weekend, and everyone seemed giddy about their holiday plans, except me. I was annoyed. I was frustrated. As I sipped my coffee I thought, "What am I missing? Why is everyone so excited? What do they know, that I don't?" I felt no passion. No anticipation. No excitement. I was emotionally numb.

Have you ever felt that way? At that time, I didn't really know what word to use to describe the way I felt. But reflecting back, I now know. I was discouraged.

Everyone will experience discouragement at one time or another. It's universal, so no one is exempt.

Discouragement seeps in quietly and slowly. The best way I can describe it is if you've ever experienced a slow leak in your car tire. The air leaks out so gradually that you don't feel the urgency to take immediate action to fix it.

It's possible to continue driving on a leaky tire for several days, all the while thinking, I'll deal with it later. But then you find yourself stranded on the side of the road forced to deal with it at the most inconvenient time.

In the same way, discouragement slowly creeps into our life. And it happens so gradually that we don't even realize its full effects until we are stranded on the side of life's highway with no more "air" left in us.

All the energy, excitement, and passion for life leaked out somewhere along the way. And suddenly, you're forced to pull over and wait for emotional roadside assistance to come rescue you. And trust me, the mental 'towing fees' are ridiculously expensive!

For months my emotional well-being had been slowly leaking. And then in the spring of 2024, I experienced an emotional "blowout" of sorts.

During this season of exhaustion and fatigue, I was simultaneously co-pastoring full-time and preaching almost every Sunday.

In March, I requested a six-week sabbatical in hopes that I could get some space to clear my head and hopefully reboot and recalibrate.

The church board graciously allowed me to take the six weeks off, but unfortunately, I would soon learn that it would take more than a six-week sabbatical to restore my soul.

One of my hardest struggles was feeling like such a hypocrite standing behind the pulpit each Sunday. I was trying to encourage the congregation and the whole time I was dealing with my own silent debilitating struggles.

I had shared my concerns and insecurities with a couple of trusted ladies in the church, but it became very evident that my secret struggles would not be safe with them.

The enemy definitely used that situation to his advantage. Their lack of discretion and complete apathy towards me pushed me deeper into my abyss. I became hopelessly convinced people would never understand or sympathize with me.

If I wanted people to love and accept me, then I would need to keep up the ridiculous charade of pretending everything was okay. Even though it clearly was not!

I felt such despair. I wanted things to be different.

Chapter 6
KEEP HOPE ALIVE

"Now faith is the substance of things hoped for...
Hebrews 11:1 KJV

Do me a favor. Say this verse out loud very slowly. Hebrews 11:1, "NOW FAITH IS THE SUBSTANCE OF THINGS HOPED FOR..."

What is faith? The substance of things hoped for.

What are you hoping for? The day you lose hope, is the day you lose your faith. Because that's what faith is. It's the substance of things hoped for.

I don't think the devil is so much out to destroy our faith, as much as he is after our hope. If he can destroy your hope, then he can sabotage your faith. Because according to Scripture, faith is the substance of things hoped for.

Without faith, it's impossible to please God. And without hope, it's impossible to have faith. That means we can't please God without hope.

In my season of discouragement, I stopped hoping.
Have you stopped hoping?
Have you stopped hoping that the best is yet to come?
Have you stopped hoping that God has more for you?
Have you stopped hoping that God's plan for your life is good?

The enemy will do everything he can to destroy your HOPE. Because faith is the substance of things hoped for.

What caused you to stop hoping?
Proverbs 13:12 NIV says, "Hope deferred makes the heart sick." What made your heart sick?

Was it the divorce?
Was it the bankruptcy?
Was it the doctor's report?
Was it the betrayal?
Was it the person who walked away and abandoned you?
Was it the death of a loved one that killed your hope?

We have a choice. We can choose to hope or choose to give up. So, choose hope. Don't allow past hurts or disappointments to cause you to forfeit the promises of God.

It takes courage to keep hoping!
I had become so discouraged that I abandoned hope.

Discouragement is, by definition, a deficit of courage.

Throughout scripture God repeatedly commands His people "to take courage" (2 Chronicles 32:7 KJV, Deuteronomy 31:6 KJV).

It's the first instruction God gave to Joshua when he called him to lead the Israelites.

Joshua 1:9 KJV, "Have I not commanded you? Be strong and courageous. Do not be afraid; do not be discouraged, for the LORD your God will be with you wherever you go."

God knew Joshua was going to face some difficult battles. That's why he commanded him, "do not be discouraged."

You and I will also face difficult battles in life. And God's instructions to us today are the same as they were to Joshua back then. "Do not be discouraged."

Let me pause here for a moment and encourage you.

Whatever battle you're facing right now, don't trust in your own strength to win it. Remember, "It's not by might, nor by power but by the Spirit of the Lord" (Zechariah 4:6 KJV).

The truth is, in our own human strength, many of the challenges we face actually are impossible. That's why we need God!

Matthew 19:26 NKJV, "But Jesus looked at them and said to them, 'With men this is impossible, but with God all things are possible.'"

Whenever you find yourself in a season of discouragement, stop focusing on what you can't do! Instead, focus on what God can do!

I love what Romans 4:18 NLT says, "Even when there was no reason for hope, Abraham kept hoping and believing..."

So, get your HOPES up. What's the best that could happen?

Chapter 7
DISCOURAGEMENT'S HALL OF FAME

"... but David encouraged himself in the Lord his God."
I Samuel 30:6 KJV

If you've ever felt discouraged, you are not alone. We see moments of discouragement all throughout the Bible.

You don't have to look far in the Word of God to find examples of Bible characters who experienced deep discouragement.

The Bible is full of people (just like you and me) who got discouraged: Elijah, Hannah, and Hagar. There was one prophet named Jeremiah who was so discouraged, he has been dubbed "the weeping prophet!"

Another Bible character is Rachel, Jacob's beloved wife. She was barren and could not conceive a child. She became so discouraged in her infertility struggles until she cried out "Give me children, or else I die" (Genesis 30:1).

Then, of course, there's Job. Has anyone ever experienced such an epic loss as Job? In one day, he lost all ten of his children, 11,000 animals, "a large number of servants," and later his own health (Job 1-2).

It's not even realistic to think you can experience that type of tragedy and loss and not get discouraged.

And how about King David? In 1 Samuel 30 KJV, there's an incident where King David became "greatly distressed and discouraged." David's own army was threatening to kill him because they blamed him for their wives and children being taken captive. David had no one to encourage him so he encouraged himself in the Lord.

Isn't it ironic that the exact same people David had encouraged, the same people David had protected, the same people David had led into battle victoriously numerous times, were the same people now threatening to kill him?

People are so fickle! One moment they're singing your praises, and the next moment they're throwing stones.

I Samuel 30:6, "David encouraged himself in the Lord." I'm very familiar with that verse. I've heard pastors preach on that verse. I've even preached from that verse myself. But I've never heard anybody preach on HOW David encouraged himself. Exactly what did David do to encourage himself? That's what I needed to know and was determined to find out.

When you find yourself discouraged, how do you encourage yourself in the Lord? Exactly what does that look like?

What are we supposed to do when we face discouragement? How do we overcome it? What steps can we take to prevent it from overwhelming us?

The purpose of this book is to hopefully address those questions and offer you some biblical insight and spiritual tips on how to overcome discouragement.

Chapter 8
RELATIONSHIPS: WHO SAID IT'S NOT PERSONAL?

Moses' arms soon became so tired he could no longer hold them up. So Aaron and Hur found a stone for him to sit on. Then they stood on each side of Moses, holding up his hands. So his hands held steady until sunset.
Exodus 17:12-13 NLT

Before we discuss how to overcome discouragement, I want to ask you a question.

What causes discouragement?
Lots of things!

The first one worth mentioning is RELATIONSHIPS!

Who hasn't been disappointed in a relationship?
All of us have.
Sometimes it's a simple misunderstanding.
Sometimes it's a blatant malicious betrayal.
That was the case with Joseph and his brothers.

Joseph's brothers blatantly betrayed him. They kidnapped him and sold him into slavery. Then they lied to their father Jacob and said he had been attacked and eaten by a wild animal!

Bruh! Who wouldn't get discouraged by that kind of betrayal?

I've never been kidnapped and sold into slavery, but I have been betrayed and lied about.

If you've been serving the Lord for very long, then you are probably already familiar with the attacks of the enemy.

You already know the enemy hates you. So, you're not surprised that he's out to destroy you. But what do you do when (like Joseph) the attacks are from your own family, friends, and inner circle?

We anticipate attacks from the enemy, but we are blindsided and unprepared when attacks come from the very ones we trusted.

The apostle Paul also experienced discouragement and disappointment in people. He mentions it in 2 Timothy 4:16-17 KJV saying, "At my first defense, no man stood with me, but all men forsook me: I pray God that it may not be laid to their charge. But the Lord stood with me, and strengthened me."

The point is, it's possible to get disappointed in people. And our disappointment can quickly turn to discouragement.

After serving on staff at the same church for 32 years, I received a significant promotion.

The Senior Lead Pastor announced during a department leader's meeting that he was beginning a transition of leadership, "a passing of the baton" to me as Lead Pastor.

My family had been a part of this church for five generations. I had faithfully served on staff for three decades. I was preaching almost every Sunday. So, from my perspective, this transition seemed like the most obvious and logical move.

I naively assumed that everyone would rejoice with me and celebrate my promotion. But I couldn't have been more wrong!

The very next morning, following that announcement, one of our staff pastors handed in his resignation. He was the first of many that would leave.

Over the next few months, 75% of our church leadership resigned and moved to other churches.

I was perplexed and confused as to why they rejected me. I even asked many of them if I had done something to upset them or offend them.

But strangely enough, every single one of them recited the same reason for their resignation. They felt "their season at our church had come to an end."

It can often be detrimental when a church congregation loses only one staff member, but to lose 12 prominent leaders (within a few months period) is potentially catastrophic!!! Some of those staff members had been with us for more than 25 years.

You can imagine my disappointment when 3/4 of the staff blatantly refused to support my leadership.

I was beyond discouraged. I felt like I had been gut-punched by some of the people I loved the most.

I considered these people to be my personal friends. I had grown up with many of them. In my mind, we were like family. What went wrong? What happened?

For the next year that followed, I would learn a very valuable and costly lesson.

Promotion comes from God alone. Stop looking to people to validate and affirm you. And sadly, don't expect everyone to celebrate you.

"For promotion cometh neither from the east, nor from the west, nor from the south. But God is the Judge: He puts down one, and exalts another" (Psalm 75:6-7 KJV).

Despite the tremendous blow to my ego, we moved forward with the transition at snail pace. The first year was bumpy. Along the way, we experienced some unexpected hiccups. But God is so faithful! Once the dust had settled the congregation began to grow exponentially.

For each person that walked away, God sent 10 families in their place. Once again proving, God can be trusted. It was also a beautiful reminder of His promise in Matthew 16:18 where He said, "I will build My church."

During this season, I experienced extreme battle fatigue. I found myself in desperate need of spiritual CPR. But again, God in his sovereignty, knew exactly what I would need. He placed a beautiful godly couple in my life named David and Alejandra. God used them in a powerful way to minister to me. Their friendship spiritually resuscitated me and gave me the encouragement I needed to keep moving forward through that season.

It's amazing to see how God places people in His body as it pleases Him (1 Corinthians 12:18 KJV).

God sovereignly positioned David and Alejandra in my life at the perfect time. They became a great source of encouragement to me. I refer to them as "my Aaron and Hur" because of the way they held up my arms when I was weak from battle fatigue (Exodus 17:12 KJV).

According to Galatians 6:2 KJV, we are instructed to "Carry each other's burdens, and in this way you will fulfill the law of Christ." I will forever be grateful to them for the way they helped carry my burdens.

Relationships are a necessary part of life. God never intended for us to isolate and do life alone. God's design, from the beginning, was for us to have community and for us to be in relationship with one another.

But, with that being said, it was never God's design for other people to replace our relationship with Him.

People are going to disappoint you. And it's not because people are evil or cruel. It's because we're human.

We were not designed to be anyone's Savior. Only Jesus Christ can fill that position.

One of the most effective ways to protect yourself from being discouraged is to keep your eyes off people and onto Jesus.

Jesus is the author and finisher of your faith. He loves you more than anyone else. Allow Him to validate you and affirm you. Place your hope and confidence in Him. He's a safe refuge.

Remember, relationships are messy! They can be a source of great encouragement, and they can also be a source of great discouragement.

If you are currently in a season of discouragement, please know it won't last forever. It's temporary. So don't be ignorant of the enemy's schemes. Every day, be on alert. Satan will try to discourage you in some way. Discouragement is a temptation "common to man" (1 Corinthians 10:13 KJV). So, don't take the bait.

Discouragement can have serious consequences. It is not to be tolerated or wallowed in. It's to be fought. If we linger in our discouragement it can be costly.

I would urge you not to make any life changing decisions while you are in a season of discouragement.

In May 2024, I reached a crossroad. I made a decision to resign and walk away from the only church family I had ever known. I also chose to walk away from my livelihood.

That decision would require me to trust God entirely with my future because I understood that I was abandoning a promising career in the ministry.

But I also knew if I continued to stay and minister under the current circumstances, I would be jeopardizing my own mental health. I do not regret resigning. But I do regret the way I handled certain things.

Few people understand the intense pressure and enormous weight that comes with pastoring a church. For me, it was the pressure to meet the demands and expectations of every parishioner. It would keep me awake at night. I would lie in bed rehearsing who I had disappointed that day.

It was as though I was living my life in "autopilot mode" and I was unable to switch into "live mode." If you've ever seen the movie "Groundhog Day" then you know what I'm talking about. Every single day is a repeat of the previous day. It feels like you're stuck in a never-ending repetitive loop. It reminds me of a hamster running in a hamster wheel. Except now, I was the hamster, and I was exhausted from spinning my wheels but going nowhere.

My parents had pastored the same congregation for 48 years. I had attended there my entire life. I had also served their ministry full-time since I was 15. Many of the congregants had watched me grow up from a small child. That church was my home. So, I was shocked and utterly disappointed when only a handful of people even reached out to check on me. Their silence spoke loudly, and it was hurtful. But it also served as a personal reminder to keep my eyes on Jesus and off people.

I do want to say thank you to the handful of people that reached out to me and offered your prayers and encouragement. You will never know what your simple acts of kindness meant to me.

Chapter 9
CIRCUMSTANCES BEYOND OUR CONTROL
*"Yet in all these things we are more than conquerors
through Him who loved us."
Romans 8:37 NKJV*

So, relationships aren't the only thing that can cause discouragement.

Another source of discouragement is LIFE CIRCUMSTANCES.

Have you ever experienced any of these circumstances?

>Death of a loved one?
>Stillbirth?
>Miscarriage?
>Bankruptcy?
>Prolonged illness?
>Infertility?
>Divorce?
>Joblessness?
>Cancer?

Sadly, I could keep going. The actual list of life circumstances is endless.

Have you ever prayed and believed for a miracle that never manifested?

I'll never forget when my mother was diagnosed with cancer. She had been sick for many months and doctors could not figure out why she was so tired and fatigued. She had lost a tremendous amount of weight, and she began to complain about severe stomach pain.

One day, she actually passed out and was admitted to the local hospital. There they did an MRI and discovered she was in the final stages of ovarian cancer.

I'll never forget the shock and disbelief I felt when I heard the doctor say the word "cancer."
I remember thinking, "That's impossible! This must be a mistake. There's no way my mother has cancer."

My mom had served the Lord her entire life.
She and my dad had faithfully co-pastored the same church for 48 years. How was it possible that she had cancer?

Although I was shocked by that diagnosis, I was not deterred. I was absolutely confident that God was going to heal her and give us a miracle.

We prayed. We fasted. We cried out to God. We added mom's name to every prayer chain we could think of. Literally hundreds of people were praying with us and standing in faith for her healing.

Despite our persistent and fervent prayers, things didn't turn out the way we hoped they would.

Mom passed away on May 24, 2021. Just 2 weeks after her diagnosis.

To say I was discouraged, would be a gross understatement. I was devastated! I have never experienced a heartbreak like that before or since.

Why did God allow this? Why didn't He heal her? He could've easily intervened. It would've been so easy for him to perform a miracle. But, he chose not to. I couldn't wrap my brain around that. I was beyond angry at God. I wanted to shake my fist in the air and scream, "How dare you!"

I've heard Christians say, "God will never disappoint you." Well... I disagree. Because God had definitely disappointed me.

It was several months after my mother's death before I attempted to trust God again. And I'm guessing I'm not the only one who has ever felt that way. I think author Lisa Terkeurst said it perfectly in the title of her new book: "I WANT TO TRUST YOU, *but I don't.*"
I lingered in that mindset of distrust for a season. But ultimately, I couldn't stay there. God had been too faithful and too good for me to stop trusting Him now.

Even Jesus Christ questioned God the Father as he hung on the cross.

We read in Mark 15:34 KJV that Jesus cried out in a loud voice, "My God, my God, why have you forsaken me?"

The last hours before His arrest and trial He cried out, "My soul is overwhelmed with sorrow to the point of death" (Mark 14:34 NIV).

If that's not discouragement, I don't know what is.

Can you imagine how discouraged the disciples must have felt after watching Jesus die on the cross?

They had forsaken all to follow Jesus. They walked away from their jobs and livelihoods for this man. They actually believed Jesus was going to set up an earthly kingdom where they would reign alongside him.

So, you can hear their disappointment in Luke 24:21 NIV when they said, "We were hoping that he was the One who was going to redeem Israel."

He was the One! The disciples just didn't see the full plan yet.

When we can't see the future and we don't know God's full plan, it's so easy to get discouraged.

God's thoughts are so much higher than ours. His ways are higher than ours.

So, in order to avoid discouragement our only option is to trust Him.

Trusting God is still a work in progress for me.
But I am learning that even when things look dark and bleak, I really can trust Him. I can trust Him even when I don't understand. I can trust Him even though I can't see the full picture.

Jesus actually warned us that in this life we would face trials and tribulations. But in that same verse (John 16:33) he also left us a promise "but be of good cheer: I have overcome the world."

Life can be so cruel, but even when we don't understand life circumstances we still have a promise. Romans 8:37 states, "Yet in all these things we are more than conquerors."

KNOW YOUR WEAPONS

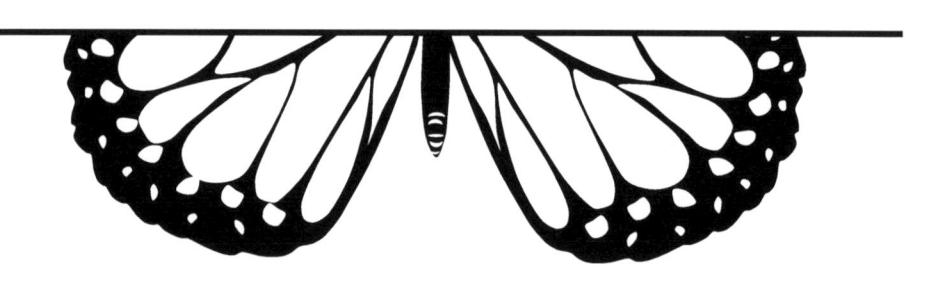

PART THREE

Chapter 10
HOPE

*"Why am I discouraged? Why is my heart so sad?
I will put my hope in God!"
Psalm 42:5 NLT*

The Bible shares many stories about men and women of God who struggled with discouragement. And there are several biblical principles we can learn from them.

The good news is that the same principles that were effective at encouraging them back then, will also be effective at encouraging us today.

For the remainder of this book, I want to present you with five weapons that we have access to as believers that can help us conquer discouragement.

These biblical principles are powerful weapons you can start using today to combat discouragement.

Oftentimes, we underestimate the power of these weapons because they're so simple. But these weapons are mighty through God, so don't devalue their effectiveness.
And remember, a weapon is only good when you choose to use it.

5 Weapons To Overcoming Discouragement

I want to start by asking you a question.
Actually, King David is the one asking the question. It's found in Psalm 42:5 NLT, "Why am I so discouraged? Why is my heart so sad?"

Can you take a moment to answer that question?

Why are you so discouraged? Why are you so sad?

Are you discouraged because you're drowning in debt?
Are you sad because your marriage is on the brink of divorce?
Are you depressed because your health is failing?
Are you disturbed because you're struggling with addictions?
Are you downcast because a relationship has gone awry?

The psalmist asks the question, "Why are you so discouraged?" But look at the words that immediately followed... "Put your hope in God" (Psalm 43:5 NLT).

The first weapon to overcoming discouragement is -
Weapon #1 - Hope in God

When you are discouraged, the first thing Scripture instructs us to do is put our hope in God.

No matter what has happened, no matter how desperate your situation looks, you can always hope in God.

Don't ever give up. Don't ever lose hope.
There is no situation too impossible for our God.

We have a choice. We can choose to hope or choose to give up. So, choose hope. Don't allow past hurts or disappointments to cause you to forfeit the promises of God.

1 Peter 1:13 NLT tells us, "Put all your hope in the gracious salvation that will come to you when Jesus Christ is revealed to the world."

And Hebrews 10:23 ESV echoes this, instructing us to "... hold fast to the confession of our hope, unwavering; for the One having promised is faithful."

Determine in your heart to always hope in God.
As long as you have JESUS - you have hope!

And like Paul prayed in Romans 15:13 NIV, "May the God of hope fill you with all joy and peace as you trust in him, so that you may overflow with hope by the power of the Holy Spirit."

We have authority to navigate our souls. We don't have to fall prey to every emotion. Even when things look impossible and hopeless - we can still choose to hope.

That's what Abraham did. Romans 4:18 NIV says, "Against all hope, Abraham in hope believed."

Make a decision today to bring yourself into alignment with God's Word and choose hope!

Chapter 11
PRAYER

"Be joyful in hope, patient in affliction, faithful in prayer."

Romans 12:12 *NIV*

The second weapon we have access to is prayer.

Weapon #2 Prayer

I realize that encouraging you to pray sounds like a cliché! But honestly, I cannot overemphasize the importance and power of prayer.

James 5:16 KJV says, "The effectual fervent prayer of a righteous man availeth much."

I can't tell you how many times I have walked into my prayer room feeling like I was carrying a 500-pound weight. But after praying (and casting my cares on God) I walked away feeling like the burden had melted away.

Prayer may not always change your circumstances, but it does give you the strength to walk through them.

Sometimes the power of prayer is really just the power to carry on. So, don't let the enemy deceive you into thinking it doesn't matter if you pray or not. Trust me, it matters!

You may be thinking, "But Gwen, I don't know how to pray. What am I supposed to say?"

Talk to God like you would talk to your best friend. He already knows how you feel, so share your frustrations and concerns with Him. He cares about what you're going through.

Whatever you do... don't stop praying! Always keep the lines of communication open between you and God.

Prayerlessness is the doorway to discouragement. When you stop praying, you throw the door wide open to discouragement.

After my mom died, I stopped praying for several days. I was angry at God. I was offended at God. I was mad at Him for not healing her the way I thought He should have. So I just stopped praying.

In my arrogance, I thought, "It's not doing any good to pray anyway. Obviously, God is going to do what He wants to do. So I'm not gonna waste my time or His by praying anymore."

Well, that was the wrong thing to do!!!

My lack of prayer sent me spiraling. My refusal to pray welcomed a spirit of discouragement into my life. In my pride and stupidity, I woke up every day and dressed myself with a garment of heaviness. By refusing to pray, I was literally welcoming depression, despair, and discouragement into my life.

I can tell you from personal experience that prayer is necessary and vital if you're going to overcome discouragement.

Very quickly I want to show you three ways prayer can help us overcome discouragement.

#1) Prayer changes our focus.
Prayer gets our focus off our circumstances and directs our gaze back onto God.
Hebrews 12:2 KJV says, "Looking unto Jesus the author and finisher of our faith…"
Psalm 121:1-2 KJV says, "I will lift up mine eyes unto the hills, from whence cometh my help. My help cometh from the Lord…"

#2) Prayer brings us closer to God.
Prayer is simply communicating with God.
James 4:8 NKJV says, "Draw near to God and He will draw near to you."
Psalm 145:18 NKJV says, "The LORD is near to all who call on him."

#3) Prayer encourages us.
This world is full of circumstances and situations that could easily discourage us. Prayer has this unique ability to restore peace and supernaturally encourage us.

When you're the most discouraged, that's when you need to pray the most.

I also want to take a moment to specifically address another level of power we can access through prayer, and that's when we pray in the Spirit.

Aren't you grateful for the Holy Spirit? I sure am!

I still remember the moment I first encountered His power and received my prayer language. I was six years old! My parents, who were pastoring the church at that time, were hosting our annual Vacation Bible School. My dad was preaching that night. I'll never forget responding to the altar call. Even at the young age of 6, I knew the power of God was real.

The moment my mom laid hands on me, she simply whispered, "Receive the Holy Spirit." And immediately, I received my prayer language. I'm 49 years old now and that recollection of me at 6 is one of my fondest memories. But it's much more than a fond memory. Receiving my prayer language was life changing!

Jesus Christ is my Savior. However, the Holy Spirit has been given to us, as a gift from God, and His purpose is to empower us.

Have you ever encountered a situation in life, and you literally did not know how to pray?

Praying in tongues allows you to pray God's perfect will even when you don't know what to pray. You can always trust the Holy Spirit to pray the perfect will of God, regardless of the situation.

Romans 8:26 NLT says "And the Holy Spirit helps us in our weakness. For example, we don't know what God wants us to pray for. But the Holy Spirit prays for us with groanings that cannot be expressed in words."

I can't explain it. I don't know how it works. I know it seems foolish in the natural, but I also know something powerful and supernatural happens when you pray in tongues.

The Baptism of the Holy Spirit is a gift available to all believers. If you have not yet unwrapped this gift, then you have no idea what you are missing!

Open your heart and your mind and ask the Lord to fill you right now. He will!

I encourage you to pray this simple prayer in faith.

Heavenly Father, I believe Your Word is true. I'm coming to you with childlike faith right now and I'm asking you to fill me with your Holy Spirit. By faith, I accept this gift.

There's a second component to prayer that many Christians often ignore. And that second ingredient is listening.

Prayer is a two-way conversation. You don't get to do all of the talking. It requires listening on your part. So, once you've talked to God, take time to listen and see what the Holy Spirit is saying to you.

Ask God to speak to you and open your spiritual eyes so you'll be able to see your circumstances from His perspective.

Prayer is a two-way dialogue. Be intentional to listen and give God priority to speak to you.

But ultimately, prayer is simply inviting God into your situation. And when you add God into the equation - anything is possible!

Chapter 12
PRAISE

"And when they began to sing and praise, the LORD set an ambush against their enemies..."
2 Chronicles 20:22 ESV

Praise is another powerful weapon we have in our arsenal.

Weapon #3 Praise

It's ironic but the moments you feel the least like worshiping will be the same moments that your worship means the most to God.

Anybody can praise God when they're on the mountain top and life is going well.

But are you able to praise God when you're walking through life's darkest valley and everything is falling apart?

If you can praise God during those moments, that's a true sacrifice of praise.

Oftentimes, it's while we are offering a sacrifice of praise, that God shows up in miraculous ways. There's a story in 2 Chronicles 20 where King Jehoshaphat is surrounded by multiple enemy armies threatening to attack God's people.

King Jehoshaphat knows God's people are outnumbered and that their situation is dire. So, he proclaims a fast throughout the land and asks the people to pray and inquire of the Lord. A prophet of the Lord speaks up and here's what he tells the people of God.

2 Chron. 20:15 & 17 NLT He said: "Listen, King Jehoshaphat and all who live in Judah and Jerusalem! This is what the Lord says to you: **'Do not be afraid or discouraged because of this vast army**. For the battle is not yours, but God's. You will not have to fight this battle. Take up your positions; stand firm and see the deliverance the Lord will give you, Judah and Jerusalem. **Do not be afraid; do not be discouraged.** Go out to face them tomorrow, and the Lord will be with you.'"

Twice, within those verses, God instructs his people not to be afraid and not to be discouraged.

He assures them that the Lord is going to deliver them! Can you guess how the Lord chose to deliver them? It was through their worship - their singing and praise!!!

In verse 21 we are told that King Jehoshaphat appoints worshipers to go out in front of the army to sing and praise the Lord. And verse 22 says, "as they began to sing and praise, the Lord sent ambushes against the enemy."

If you are being threatened by the enemy of discouragement, then I urge you to offer up a sacrifice of praise.

God cannot resist the sweet fragrance of extravagant worship. As you begin to offer up your costly praise, don't be surprised when the Lord sends ambushes against your enemies.

Another Bible story that beautifully depicts the power of praise is found in Acts 16. It tells about Paul and Silas being held in prison and bound up with chains.

Acts 16:25 KJV: "And at midnight Paul and Silas prayed, and sang praises unto God: and the prisoners heard them."

Acts 16:26 NIV: "Suddenly there was such a violent earthquake that the foundations of the prison were shaken. At once all the prison doors flew open, and everyone's chains came loose."

Look at verse 25 and notice the two things that Paul and Silas did to warrant such a supernatural response from God. They prayed and sang praises to God.

Two very simple acts of praying and singing praises caused the miraculous to be unleashed.

It's a powerful reminder from 2 Corinthians 10:4 NKJV, "The weapons of our warfare are not carnal."

As Christians, we do not fight our battles with worldly methods.

Paul and Silas did not start a riot within jail. They did not insult and curse the prison guards. They did not harass their fellow prisoners. They simply prayed and sang praises to God.

And then God showed up and performed miracles on their behalf.

Now this is what's interesting. Paul and Silas were in an actual prison bound with literal chains. But there are countless saints being held captive in an invisible prison of hopelessness. They are bound with demonic chains of discouragement and depression.

Praise has the power to break those chains and open prison doors. Praise is one of the most effective weapons we have against discouragement.

It would be foolish for us to ignore this mighty weapon.

Psalm 34:1 CSB, "His praise will ever be on my lips."

Chapter 13
REST

"This is the resting place, let the weary rest..."
Isaiah 28:12 NIV

The fourth weapon I want to mention is rest.

Weapon #4 Rest

It seems ironic and counterintuitive that rest would be a weapon. But rest is so important that God Himself modeled it for us during creation when He rested on the seventh day.

Rest is also such a priority to God that He mentions it fourth on the list of The Ten Commandments.

As believers, we would not fathom breaking the 10 Commandments when it comes to murder or stealing or committing adultery.

But we think nothing of breaking the fourth commandment which instructs us to treat the Sabbath as a day of rest, both physically and mentally.

Jeremiah 31:25 BSB says, "I will refresh the weary soul and replenish all who are weak."

As I mentioned earlier, I love to drink coffee every morning while sitting outside in the screen porch.

There have been a few occasions where the screen door was left open and little birds have accidentally wandered inside.

That's not a huge problem, except for the fact that I own a chocolate Labrador that loves to eat birds!

I know that if I don't get those little birds safely outside the screen porch quick enough, then my dog will have no mercy when it comes to capturing them and devouring them.

On one occasion, there was a particular little bird that had gotten caught inside the porch area. I tried and tried to shew that little bird out the door. But each time I got close, it would outmaneuver me and fly past me to the opposite end of the porch.

This went on for at least 15 minutes as I chased that little bird all over the porch. I had never seen a bird actually panting until that day.

But finally, it grew so exhausted that it simply couldn't fly anymore.

I quickly scooped him up, carried him outside, and safely released him to the open sky.

Here's my point. The entire time that I was trying to rescue the bird, it was running away from me.

The bird didn't know that I was trying to save him from my dog that wanted to eat him alive.

From the bird's point of view, I was the enemy!

How many of us are like that bird?
God is trying to protect us from an enemy who wants to devour us. But we keep running away from God, not realizing His intentions for us are good!

God is trying to rescue us. He wants to scoop us up and place us safely in the palm of his hand.

God is saying, "Please trust me. I know things you don't know. There is an enemy trying to devour you. Please let me help you."

But we are foolishly determined to keep maneuvering away from the very person who can save us.

Jesus said, "Come to me, all of you who are weary and carry heavy burdens, and I will give you rest" (Matthew 11:28 KJV).

Does your soul need rest?

So many of us are exhausted because we are fluttering around, trying to figure things out on our own. We are trying to solve this problem and fix that issue.

The whole time God is actively pursuing us saying, "I want to help you. Please come to me."

Isaiah 28:12 NLT says, "Here is a place of rest; let the weary rest here. But the people would not listen."

As long as you're doing life in your own strength, you're going to be frustrated and exhausted. And that leads to discouragement.

If you're tired of being tired, and your soul is weary and worn out then I invite you to find rest in Jesus today.

God knows things you don't know.
God sees things you can't see.

We see impossibilities. We see medical reports that aren't good. We see dead ends. We see all the reasons why it won't work. We see things in the natural. But God is supernatural!

God is able to make a way where there is no way. Don't forget to add Him into your equation. God is the game-changer!

You don't have to go through life exhausted and discouraged. There is rest for the weary.

Chapter 14
THE WORD OF GOD

"For the word of God is alive and powerful. It is sharper than the sharpest two-edged sword..."
Hebrews 4:12 NLT

Last but not least... the fifth weapon in our arsenal to fight discouragement is the Word of God.

Weapon #5 Word of God

The Bible is a book like no other. It's the infallible Word of God. It is a blueprint for your life. It's better than any self-help book you can buy.

The Bible is NOT just a book of stories and rules. It has supernatural power to give us hope and encouragement.

The Bible is a lamp to our feet and a light to our path (Psalm 119:105 KJV). God's Word has this supernatural ability to illuminate the way for us. It provides us with direction, instruction, and guidance.

If you are struggling with discouragement, then dive deep into the Word of God. The goal of reading, learning, and studying the Bible is to build our faith.

Romans 15:4 NLT, "...the Scriptures give us hope and encouragement as we wait patiently for God's promises to be fulfilled."

The Bible hasn't lost its power or relevance. God's Word is every bit as powerful today as it has always been. We simply must learn how to access its power.

The Bible contains some powerful promises, and they're all ours when we believe the Word and commit to living according to it.

Never underestimate the power of God's Word.

The fact is, the Word of God has the power and ability to impact every area of our lives, but only if we allow it to.

Read it, study it, love it, and live it! God's Word is a powerful weapon against discouragement.

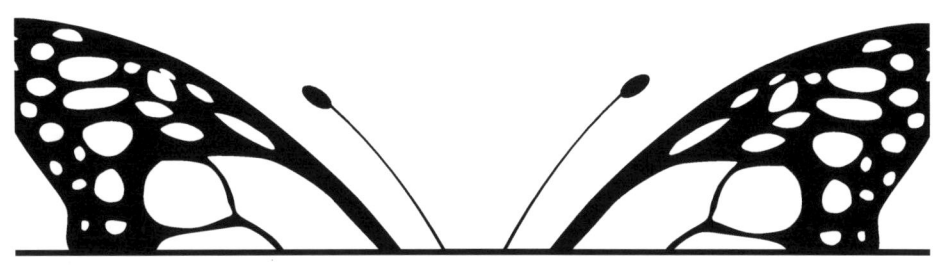

GOD AIN'T FINISHED
PART FOUR

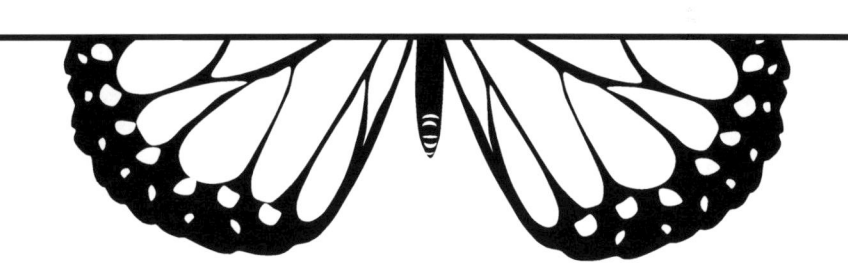

Chapter 15
COURAGE FOR THE DISCOURAGED

*This is my command—be strong and courageous!
Do not be afraid or discouraged. For the LORD your
God is with you wherever you go."*
Joshua 1:9 NLT

Now that you've reached the end of the book, I hope you feel more equipped and prepared when it comes to conquering discouragement.

Stay on guard! Discouragement is always crouching at the door of your heart, ready to sneak in, if you allow it.

In the same way that discouragement is contagious, so is encouragement. So, find a Bible-believing church and get your face in that place!

It is vital that you surround yourself with a godly community!

Don't allow discouragement to stop you from moving forward into the good things God has prepared for you.

Now that you know the enemy's tactics and strategies, you can armor up more effectively.

Remember: don't fight this battle in your own strength.

Use the weapons we discussed in the book. They may seem silly in the natural but they are mighty through God!

Let's recap the weapons:

    1. Hope
    2. Prayer
    3. Praise
    4. Rest
    5. God's Word

God doesn't work the way we expect him to or how or when we want him to. So, whenever you start feeling discouraged, choose to trust that He simply has a different and better plan for you.

Trust His timing.
Trust His goodness.
Trust His faithfulness

God is not finished with you! Your best days are still ahead! So, empty out the negative, let go of the old, and make room for all that God wants to do in your life!

Philippians 1:6 NLT, "I am certain that God, who began the good work within you, will continue his work until it is finally finished on the day when Christ Jesus returns."

I'd like to close out this book by praying for you.

In the name of Jesus, I come against every spirit of discouragement. I come against every spirit of despair, hopelessness, fear, despondency, and depression.

In the name of Jesus, I come against feelings of failure, thoughts of quitting, thoughts of giving up, and thoughts of suicide.

I declare that God is greater than any discouragement we face. I call on the power of Jesus Christ, and I release new faith, new hope, new vision, new confidence, new determination, new zeal, and new enthusiasm.

Holy Spirit, come baptize us, saturate us, marinate us, infuse us with courage, faith, hope, and love!

Lord Jesus, I still believe you will complete the work you started.

Amen.

Dear Readers,

I am writing to express my sincere gratitude for your interest in and support of my book, "Courage for the Discouraged." It means the world to me that you have taken the time to read and engage with my work.

Your kind words, thoughtful feedback, and encouragement have been a tremendous source of inspiration. Knowing that my words have resonated with you and provided comfort, strength, or even a spark of hope has filled my heart with joy.

I believe that everyone faces moments of discouragement in their lives. My hope is that this book has offered you a path to find courage, strength, and resilience in the face of adversity.

Thank you again for your support.
May God bless you.

—Gwen

PRISCILLA GWEN ENGLAND

GET TO KNOW THE AUTHOR

Gwen England is a graduate of Austin College with a BA in Communications. She is also a licensed minister with the Assemblies of God.

Beyond her academic achievements and ministerial credentials, Gwen possesses a unique anointing that sets her apart. When she preaches, her words resonate deeply, touching the hearts of listeners in a profound way. It's evident that her ministry is fueled by more than just intellect or experience; it's a divine calling, empowered by the Holy Spirit.

Gwen has been in full-time ministry for over three decades. Her dedication to the Lord has been unwavering. During that time, she has served in various roles and capacities including: worship pastor, executive pastor, co-lead pastor, teacher, and mentor. With the many titles and positions she has held throughout her ministry career, the one she cherishes most is follower of Christ.

Gwen's ministry is marked by her passion for sharing the Gospel and her commitment to seeing lives transformed. Through her preaching and teaching she has witnessed countless individuals come to know Jesus. Her ability to connect with people on a personal level and her unwavering belief in God's power to heal and restore have made her a beloved figure in the ministry community.

PRISCILLA GWEN ENGLAND

SCAN HERE FOR MORE INFO

notes   DATE   /   /

notes   DATE   /   /

notes

DATE   /   /

notes   DATE   /   /

notes

DATE   /   /

notes DATE / /

notes　　　　　　　　　　　　　DATE　　　/　　　/

notes   DATE   /   /

notes

DATE   /   /

notes

DATE   /   /

notes

DATE   /   /

notes

DATE   /   /

notes   DATE   /   /

notes DATE / /

notes

DATE   /   /

notes

DATE   /   /

notes

DATE / /

notes

DATE   /   /

notes

DATE / /

notes

DATE   /   /

notes

DATE   /   /

notes

DATE   /   /